YOU CHOOSE
BOOKS™

THE VIETNAM WAR

AN INTERACTIVE MODERN HISTORY ADVENTURE

by Michael Burgan

Consultant:
Marc Leepson, Editor
*Webster's World Dictionary
of the Vietnam War*

CAPSTONE PRESS
a capstone imprint

You Choose Books are published by Capstone Press,
1710 Roe Crest Drive, North Mankato, Minnesota 56003
www.capstonepub.com

Library of Congress Cataloging-in-Publication Data
Burgan, Michael, author.
  The Vietnam War : an interactive modern history adventure / by Michael Burgan.
    pages cm — (You choose. Modern history)
  Summary: "Explores various perspectives on the Vietnam War and those involved in it.
The reader's choices reveal the historical details"— Provided by publisher.
  Includes bibliographical references and index.
  ISBN 978-1-4765-4187-7 (library binding)
  ISBN 978-1-4765-5218-7 (paperback)
  ISBN 978-1-4765-6064-9 (ebook PDF)
  1. Vietnam War, 1961-1975—Juvenile literature. I. Title.
  DS557.7.B895 2014
  959.704'3—dc23   2013032520

Editorial Credits
Mandy Robbins, editor; Gene Bentdahl, designer; Wanda Winch, media researcher;
Danielle Ceminsky, production specialist

Photo Credits
AP Images, 19, 30, 53, 63, 83, Horst Faas, 21, 29, 44, 56, LM, 47; Capstone, 10; Corbis:
Bettmann, 6, Science Faction/William James Warren, 93, Sygma/Jacques Pavlovsky,
105, Wally McNamee, 12; Courtesy of Anthony Chliek, 99; Getty Images Inc: AFP,
74, Time & Life Pictures/Charles H. Phillips, 87; Lyndon Baines Johnson Library,
37; Shutterstock: Andre Viegas, paper background, Dimec, camo background design;
SuperStock Inc: Everest Collection, 100; U.S. Air Force photo, 69; U.S. Army: SSG
Howard C. Breedlove, cover

Printed in the United States of America in North Mankato, Minnesota.
062015   009049R

TABLE OF CONTENTS

ABOUT YOUR ADVENTURE

YOU are living through one of the worst wars in U.S. history. The center of the conflict is in Vietnam, but fighting also takes place in the neighboring countries of Laos and Cambodia.

In this book you'll explore how the choices people made meant the difference between life and death. The events you'll experience happened to real people.

Chapter One sets the scene. Then you choose which path to take. Follow the directions at the bottom of each page. The choices you make will change your outcome. After you finish one path, go back and read the others for new perspectives and more adventures.

YOU CHOOSE the path
you take through history.

Ho Chi Minh became leader of North Vietnam after World War II.

War in Vietnam

Vietnam was once part of a colony of France called Indochina. Vietnam declared independence in 1945, with Ho Chi Minh as its leader. But the French wouldn't give up their colony. In 1946 a war began that lasted until 1954. The Vietnamese won the war and their independence.

The United States supported France against Vietnam. After World War II (1939–1945) the Cold War had begun, as the United States and the Soviet Union competed for power. The Soviets wanted to spread communism around the world. Americans wanted to stop the spread of communism because it denied people's political and economic freedom. Ho Chi Minh wanted Vietnam to be a Communist country.

7

Turn the page.

When the war with France ended, Vietnam was split. Ho's Communist government controlled the north, while a government friendly to the United States controlled the south. The U.S. government wanted to keep South Vietnam out of Communist hands.

North Vietnam supported the National Liberation Front (NLF), a political group in the south. The NLF's military wing was called the Viet Cong. The NLF wanted to unite the country under Ho. In 1959 the Viet Cong launched a war against South Vietnam.

Meanwhile, the United States had been supporting South Vietnam since it was formed in 1954. The U.S. provided money and military training. By 1963 about 16,000 military troops were there acting as advisers to the South Vietnamese military in its fight against the Viet Cong.

President Lyndon Johnson sent the first American ground combat forces to South Vietnam in 1965. Within three years the number had increased to 536,000. By then North Vietnamese troops were actively working with the Viet Cong to fight the Americans and the South Vietnamese. Meanwhile, the Soviet Union and the Communist nation of China sent billions of dollars in aid and weapons to North Vietnam.

For Americans, the Vietnam War presented several challenges. TV crews went to the battlefield. Some Americans were shocked to see the violence of the war on TV.

Some people began to protest what they saw as an immoral war. Others supported the country's military role in Vietnam, believing in the need to fight communism.

Turn the page.

Paris Peace Accords cease-fire,
January 27, 1973
Land held by North Vietnam's army
Land held by South Vietnam's army
Land held by Viet Cong

10

Many young people fought and died on all sides in the Vietnam War. You will have to decide whether to take part in the war. You could be forced to kill the enemy—or face being killed.

To be an American who volunteers to fight, go to page **13**.

To be a South Vietnamese teen who's not sure which side to support, go to page **45**.

To be a young American who opposes the war, go to page **75**.

Marine recruits march in step during boot camp training.

CHAPTER 2

Serving Your Country

It's 1965, and you've been in college for two years. But you want to volunteer for the Marines. Your father was a Marine during World War II, and you want to serve your country too. You convince your friend John to enlist with you.

The Marines accept you both. You travel to San Diego, California, for boot camp. After boot camp, you receive more training. One day you are asked to join an aviation unit. You assumed you would be in the infantry, like John is. But it could be exciting to learn how to work with helicopters and maybe even fly in them.

13

To work with helicopters, turn to page **14**.

To stay in the infantry, turn to page **17**.

"I'll give the helicopters a try," you say.

You tell John your decision. He wishes you well as you leave for more training in Tennessee. There you learn all about the engines that keep the "choppers" flying. You also learn that if you go to Vietnam, you won't just fix engines. There is a good possibility you'll be part of a helicopter crew, and maybe fire one of its guns at the enemy below.

As the summer of 1965 approaches, you finish your training. By now thousands of Marines have been sent to South Vietnam, and you receive orders to go too. You'll be part of a Marine Air Group based at Chu Lai. Your title is crew chief.

You use your new skills to keep the helicopters in top shape. The Marines use a helicopter known as a Huey. Various types of Hueys are used to bring troops and supplies into battle, rescue wounded Marines, and attack enemy positions.

Word spreads in August 1965 that the Viet Cong have bases near Chu Lai. The U.S. generals in the region plan an attack.

One of your new buddies is a pilot named Stu. "Are you ready to go out and kill some VC?" he asks. VC is slang for the Viet Cong. Some American troops also call them "Charlie."

15

"I'm ready to do whatever I have to do for my country," you say.

Turn the page.

Your commanding officer talks to your squadron on August 17. He explains that choppers will be taking troops to three landing zones. Gunships will also be used to attack the VC. Finally, some helicopters will be used as medevacs—they'll come in to pick up the wounded. You've had some training for those missions too. The medevac flights have a pilot, co-pilot, medic, and a crew chief. As the crew chief on a medevac, you would help the medic bring the wounded on board.

The officer looks at you. "Do you care which kind of bird you'll be on?"

Stu will be flying a Huey taking troops into the battle zone. You'd like to go with him. But you like the idea of rescuing the wounded too.

To go on a transport flight, turn to page **20.**

To go on a medevac flight, turn to page **30.**

The sergeant is glad that you want to do the hard work of a "grunt." You finish your training at the end of 1965. The first Marines have landed in South Vietnam and more keep arriving. Finally, you and John get your assignments. You're both part of the 3rd Battalion, 4th Marines. Soon you make the long journey from the United States to a Marine base at Da Nang, South Vietnam. South Vietnamese troops are also based there.

You learn how some of the Vietnamese live. Many of them work at Da Nang and other U.S. bases. At night shells fired from some of their villages land near the base.

"Why are they firing at us?" you ask your sergeant, named Rizzo.

"There are VC there and in most of the villages around here," he says. "And now the NVA are coming into the area too." NVA stands for North Vietnamese Army. They are well-equipped forces from North Vietnam fighting with the Viet Cong.

The Marine commanders are trying to win the support of the civilians. The goal is to convince the local people that the United States will help protect them from the VC and improve their lives.

"We're starting a new program," Rizzo tells you. "It's called County Fair, part of the CAP, the Marines' Combined Action Program. Do you want to take part?"

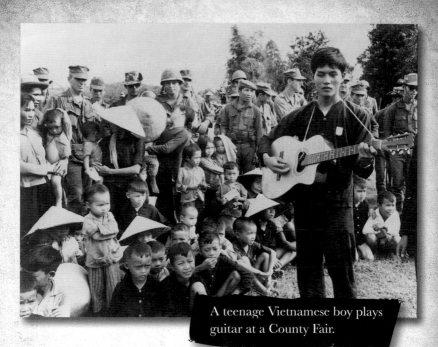

A teenage Vietnamese boy plays guitar at a County Fair.

You want to help win what some Americans call "the hearts and minds" of the South Vietnamese. But the rest of your company is about to head north. It would be good to stick with your buddies.

To take part in County Fair, turn to page **24.**

To stay with your company and go north, turn to page **40.**

19

"I'd like to go on Stu's chopper," you say.

The battle begins just after 6 a.m. Marine planes drop napalm, a chemical that burns flesh. Artillery rounds also blast the site. The idea is to clear an area where the helicopters can safely land with the troops. At your base nine Marines armed for battle enter your Huey, and you take your place by the door gun. One by one, the choppers leave the base at Chu Lai and head out to look for the Viet Cong bases.

The Huey's huge blades sound like the fast beating of a drum. You feel your heart pounding almost as fast inside your chest. You smell the jet fuel that powers the engine. You've flown in a Huey plenty of times, and you have lots of training with its M-60 machine gun, but this is your first taste of combat. You wonder if the other guys are as afraid as you are.

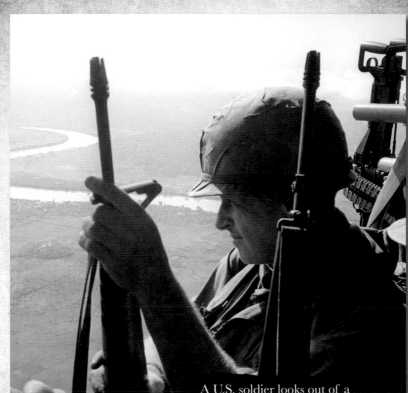

A U.S. soldier looks out of a helicopter at Vietnam.

Turn the page.

Around 8 a.m. your chopper approaches the landing zone (LZ) and then touches the ground. The Marines leave the chopper, and you're thankful there was no enemy fire. Now the chopper takes off, and you head back to pick up more Marines.

Things are different the next time you reach the landing site. The Viet Cong are firing at incoming helicopters. You aim your gun where the enemy fire is coming from. You shoot, never knowing if you're hitting anyone.

As you head back, a radio message comes in from the base. A village nearby may have Viet Cong hiding in it. Some Marines have already been sent there to check. Stu now turns your helicopter toward the village.

From your open door, you see women and children running from the village.

"Are you going to fire?" Stu asks.

"I can't shoot women and kids," you say.

"If that village supports the VC, then those civilians are VC," Stu says. "Our orders are to kill Charlie whenever we see him."

Stu outranks you, and he has his orders to follow. All Marines have to obey orders or risk being court-martialed. But you are only required to follow a lawful order. Is it lawful to kill civilians who aren't trying to harm you?

23

To fire on the civilians, turn to page **27.**

To refuse to fire, turn to page **33.**

"Sir, I'd love to help the local people."

"You'll be hunting for VC too," Rizzo says.

The next day you and other Marines go with South Vietnamese troops to a nearby village. Town leaders say the VC have been forcing them to let the guerrillas use the village as a base. South Vietnamese troops round up residents and issue them ID cards. Meanwhile, a Marine band and local musicians entertain the people.

"The idea is to make it fun, like a county fair," Rizzo says. "We also give medical treatment to anyone who needs it."

Over the next few weeks, you go out on several of the County Fair operations. One of the Marines' duties is to protect the South Vietnamese troops. On one mission the fair is interrupted by mortar shells exploding nearby.

"Incoming!" someone yells, and you hide behind a mound of dirt. As the mortars fall from the skies, you hear the sound of machine guns. A corporal with a radio calls back to the base to ask for helicopters to attack the enemy. You look up and see Rizzo ordering the other men to find safe positions. Bullets rip through the trees around him, and one finds its target. Rizzo falls. Someone has to try to help him. It's the Marine way.

You start to stand, your M-14 rifle is up and ready to fire.

"Get down!" the radioman yells.

"I have to get the sergeant," you say.

"There's VC everywhere," the radioman replies. "We should wait."

Turn the page.

You know the situation is bad. But Rizzo could be dying from a wound while you wait for the helicopters.

To try to rescue Rizzo, turn to page **35.**

To wait for the helicopters, turn to page **38.**

"I don't like this," you say, "but I'll follow the orders."

You begin firing. But no one ordered you to aim correctly. You fire over the civilians' heads.

Stu circles around the village. Suddenly you feel a jolt as the Huey is hit by enemy machine gun fire.

"We're going down!" Stu yells. The nose of the chopper starts to drop. Stu tries to keep the helicopter from crashing, and he manages to keep it level. But he's lost control, and the chopper lands hard. You slam into the helicopter's gun.

27

Turn the page.

"My arm!" you cry, as your left arm crashes into the M-60 at a bad angle. You're sure it must be broken. Luckily, another Huey saw your aircraft take a hit. The second helicopter slowly lands, its blades kicking up dust as they spin. You hear explosions and the sound of machine guns as a Marine runs over from the second chopper.

"Let's get you back to base," the Marine says. You, Stu, and the co-pilot run for the chopper. Soon it's in the air and heading back to base. With any luck, your arm will be fixed up and you'll be back on the job soon. But you hope you never get another order to fire at civilians.

THE END

To follow another path, turn to page 11.
To read the conclusion, turn to page 101.

Marines treat their wounded on a battlefield in Vietnam.

"I'll go on the medevac," you say. You tell Stu, then find the rest of your new crew. The corpsman, George, has stocked the Huey with bandages and other medical supplies. Several hours after the first transport choppers left for the battle, the call comes for your medevac to go to the scene.

A wounded Marine is loaded into a medevac helicopter.

As you approach the fighting, you hear the sounds of artillery and smaller guns. Bill, the pilot, hovers over a group of Marines who have had casualties. He lands the chopper, and you help George get the wounded men onto it. Even before you lift off, George is treating the injured. He wraps bleeding wounds and gives the men medicine to kill their pain. Soon you are speeding off to the hospital at Chu Lai.

The battle goes on all through the day, and your chopper flies several more missions. You feel your stomach churn as you see horrendous injuries, such as arms and legs blown off.

"I try not to look," Bill tells you as you make your fourth trip out. "Seeing all that blood and guts might make it too hard for me to fly this thing."

Turn the page.

You land and begin helping George with the next group of injured men. Back in the air, you hear gunfire—and it's close to your Huey! More shots come, and dozens of them rip into the chopper. George slumps down as one of the bullets hits him in the head. As you go to help him, the helicopter starts to spin wildly.

"I can't control it," Bill says. "We're going down!"

You think about your family back home and all you had hoped to do when you got back from Vietnam. But the helicopter crashes hard, and you die instantly.

32

THE END

To follow another path, turn to page 11.
To read the conclusion, turn to page 101.

"I can't fire on kids, Stu."

"Listen up," he says angrily, "are you disobeying an order?"

"I'm not sure it's a lawful order. I won't fire."

But the gunners in nearby helicopters are firing. Your stomach tightens as you see some of the running women fall down. You've heard stories about women who support the VC attacking American troops. But the people running below you don't look armed or dangerous. How could anyone kill them?

Stu doesn't say a word as he heads back to Chu Lai. When you land, you go to the commanding officer and explain what happened.

Turn the page.

"Son," he says, "those civilians didn't have weapons—today. But they could go back to their village and help kill Americans tomorrow."

You realize now that this war isn't like most wars Americans have fought. You can't tell the enemy from the civilians. But you're not sure you'll ever accept the idea of killing civilians—especially if you never know if they support the enemy.

THE END

To follow another path, turn to page 11.
To read the conclusion, turn to page 101.

You rush toward Rizzo's body. The other Marines see you and increase their fire at the VC. You see that the sergeant is bleeding from his arm and his chest.

"Go back," Rizzo says breathing heavily.

"Can't, Sarge." Before you grab his body, you throw a grenade at an area where a lot of enemy fire seems to be coming from. You wait for the explosion. The firing stops. You hit your target!

But bullets continue to whiz around you as you drag Rizzo to safety. You look up and see several Marine helicopters. One is a gunship. Another is a medevac, with medical staff on board.

Turn the page.

The medevac lands in a field nearby. The corpsman and a Marine rush out with a stretcher and put Rizzo on it. As they take him away, you turn and see something sailing toward you. It's a VC grenade!

You duck, but it explodes just 10 feet away from you. The blast sends you flying. When you land, you're dazed, and something's wrong with your right leg. Touching your knee, you feel blood. You look down, and part of your leg is missing! Just before you pass out, you realize you'll be joining Rizzo on the medevac—and soon you'll be going back to the United States.

THE END

To follow another path, turn to page 11.
To read the conclusion, turn to page 101.

President Johnson (right) visited wounded Vietnam War veterans in the hospital.

You crouch back down behind the mound. Both sides are shooting, while the VC fire more mortar shells. In a few minutes, you hear the sound of approaching helicopters. The Marines now have more firepower than the enemy does, and the company begins to move forward. You and another Marine run over to Rizzo.

"I'm all right," he says. "It's not so bad."

The other Marine stays with the sergeant to wait for a helicopter to pick him up. Looking ahead, you see many of the VC running away. You go after them, pausing every now and then to fire your rifle. After one round you see a VC in the distance stagger and fall. You got him! As the gunships drive off the rest of the enemy, you run toward the downed VC. The battlefield is quiet now.

You stand above the enemy soldier. He's not much older than a kid in junior high school. He lies there with a wounded leg. The medevac will take him back to Da Nang too. You've survived your first battle and captured a prisoner. But you know there will be more battles to come. Next time you and Rizzo might not be so lucky.

THE END

To follow another path, turn to page 11.
To read the conclusion, turn to page 101.

"I want to stay with the company," you say, looking at John. He smiles.

You're taking part in Operation Hastings. The U.S. commanders want to stop the North Vietnamese from launching a major invasion. Your company is part of the first wave of Marines to land near the NVA position on July 15.

"Hear that?" John says to you over the whir of the chopper blades. "They're shooting at us. We're going into a hot LZ."

You listen to the machine gun fire, frightened about facing combat for the first time. But you have a job to do, and you're ready to do it.

The Marines call for artillery to attack the NVA, and the enemy fire finally stops. You and other companies receive an order to take a nearby hill. You've gone only a short way when NVA mortar shells begin to land all around you.

"Be care—," John starts to say to you, but before he can finish, enemy machine gun fire cuts him down. You want to cry, seeing your good friend die in front of you. But before you can do anything, an enemy bullet pierces your right shoulder. You fall to your knees.

"Pull back!" your sergeant says, as a massive NVA force begins to swarm toward your company.

Turn the page.

As you struggle to stand, artillery fire from the Marines begins to hit the advancing enemy. The NVA duck for cover, and in that moment you start to run. In a second, you feel another bullet hit you in the leg, and then another. You fall again. The artillery shelling stops.

The Marine gunners must think they've wiped everyone out, or else are running low on ammo. You hear a noise behind you. You can turn just enough to see three enemy soldiers approaching. They gesture for you to get up. They're not going to kill you—they want to take you prisoner!

You've heard the stories about what happens to American POWs. You'll be lucky if the North Vietnamese treat your wounds. And most likely they'll torture you.

You'll have to be strong and try to escape the prison camp if you can. With some luck, you can still survive the war and get home to see your loved ones again.

THE END

To follow another path, turn to page 11.
To read the conclusion, turn to page 101.

South Vietnamese president Ngo Dinh Diem inspects his troops.

CHAPTER 3

Which Side?

You are a teenager living in a small village not far from Saigon, the capital of South Vietnam. For generations, your Buddhist relatives have grown rice here. It's early in 1963, and your family has been touched by the long wars that have divided Vietnam. Your uncle supports Ho Chi Minh and isn't shy about saying so. Your brother is a soldier in South Vietnam's army, which is known as the Army of the Republic of Vietnam (ARVN). He's fighting the Viet Cong.   45

The fighting is spreading, and South Vietnam needs more soldiers. President Ngo Dinh Diem has called for all men younger than 28 who have graduated from high school to receive basic military training.

Turn the page.

You never finished high school, because your parents needed your help on the farm. But you see troops stationed nearby. Some are Buddhist, like you. Others are Roman Catholic, like President Diem. Your father worries about the spreading violence. The Viet Cong threaten local farmers to give them help or be killed. One day your father says to you, "It's not safe for you here. We want you to go to Saigon to live with your aunt."

"But what about the farm?" you ask. And all your friends are here in the village. But then you think that it might be exciting to live in a big city like Saigon.

To go to Saigon, turn to page **48.**

To stay in the village, turn to page **51.**

The city of Saigon, lit up for the Vietnamese New Year celebration

Your parents and your little brother, Bao, cry and hug you as you prepare to go. Soon you've packed your clothes, and you climb into a wagon. It takes you to the nearest bus station, and you begin your trip to Saigon. In the capital the streets are filled with cars and taxis rushing by. You reach your Aunt Ly's house and ask her what people in Saigon think of the war.

"Oh, we're not bothered by it much here," she says. "Most of the fighting is far away."

One day in June, you are shocked as you hear Ly talking about something she read in the paper.

"A Buddhist monk set himself on fire yesterday!" she tells you. "He was protesting the policies of President Diem."

She explains that Diem favors the small minority of Catholics in the country over the Buddhists, who make up the majority. And government troops recently killed some Buddhists who were demanding their religious freedom.

Ly says, "Diem only wants power and money for him, his family, and his supporters."

Your parents decided you should go back to school in Saigon. One day you hear some of the older students talking about Diem.

"He's a tyrant," one says. "My older brother is working with the Viet Cong to end his rule."

"But the Communists are no better," another boy protests. "They kill innocent people all the time."

Turn the page.

"They only kill people who won't fight against Diem," the first boy says. "I want to help the Viet Cong." He turns to you. "What about you? Will you help us fight Diem?"

You don't like that Diem orders attacks on Buddhists. But you're not sure it's right to leave school to fight the government.

To go with the other student, turn to page **59.**

To stay in school, turn to page **54.**

"I should stay here in the village to help you if the fighting gets worse," you say.

To try to protect the villages in your area, the government has created what it calls strategic hamlets. South Vietnam receives money from the United States to carry out this plan. The government clears land in areas where it's easier for the ARVN to defend citizens.

A group of soldiers forces your family into this new village. The strategic hamlet feels more like a prison, with barbed wire surrounding the homes and farmland. The government keeps troops in the village for part of the year. When the rainy season comes, the ARVN pull back to their main bases. The soldiers give you and other men guns. "If the Viet Cong come back," an officer says, "you'll have to defend yourselves."

51

Turn the page.

For a couple years you and your family live safely in the strategic hamlet. But one rainy season, you see armed men approaching the village.

"Viet Cong!" your father says. The men of the village had already agreed they would not fight if the Communists came to the village. It's better to not resist them than risk having everyone killed. The Viet Cong gather all the men in the center of the village.

"Look at what the government does to us," one of the Viet Cong leaders says. "They force us off our land and put us behind barbed wire. Is that any way to live? Join us, and bring justice and equality to South Vietnam!"

You hate that the government forced you from your home. But could you fight your own government? After all, your brother is in the ARVN. Even so, you're tired of foreigners trying to control Vietnam.

To stay in the village, turn to page **66.**

To go with the Viet Cong, turn to page **57.**

South Vietnamese flee their village as it is being bombed.

53

"I'm here to study, not fight," you say.

One boy sneers at you, "Coward. You can't escape the war. If you end up fighting for the government, you'll see how strong the Viet Cong are."

You go home but don't tell Aunt Ly what happened. Let her keep thinking the war is far away. You work hard in school, but life in South Vietnam slowly gets worse. Generals who dislike President Diem kill him. But the new leaders are no better at running the government or fighting the war. Then, when you finish school, you begin military training as required. Soon you are sent into the countryside to fight the Viet Cong.

More American soldiers arrive to help South Vietnam fight the Communists starting in March 1965. Some of them work with your unit.

You learn a few words of English, but you sense the Americans don't really like the Vietnamese. You hear that some GIs tease Vietnamese girls. They also boss around the ARVN soldiers. But you follow your orders like you were trained to do.

You fight in several battles in the countryside. You see the blackened ground from bombs dropped by American planes. Many trees have had their leaves stripped off by a chemical called Agent Orange. You also see civilians killed by the war. You hope your country's suffering will end soon.

As the fighting goes on, you pick up skills as a medic. One day an ARVN captain approaches you and asks if you would like to get more medical training back in Saigon.

Turn the page.

A South Vietnamese soldier captures a Viet Cong fighter.

You like the idea of getting out of the muddy battlefield and going back to Saigon. And you would get more pay. But you're not sure you want to spend every day seeing horribly wounded soldiers.

To stay with your unit, turn to page **62.**

To go back to Saigon for training, turn to page **64.**

You think about your uncle, who supports Ho Chi Minh and the Communists. Years before, Ho took land from the rich and gave it to poor farmers. You like the idea of the government helping the poor—not forcing them from their homes.

"I'll go with you," you tell the leader. Several other young men say they'll go too. The leader smiles as you kiss your parents good-bye and head off with the Communist troops.

The Viet Cong take you to a training school for guerrillas. The school is deep in the jungles of South Vietnam. As a guerrilla, you'll carry light weapons and strike villages or enemy bases and patrols quickly, then pull back to safety. Some of your weapons were captured from the Americans.

57

Turn the page.

You learn that troops from North Vietnam are helping the Viet Cong. The captain of your unit says the North Vietnamese want men to work along the Ho Chi Minh Trail. North Vietnamese built this network of trails through Cambodia and Laos to move supplies from the north to the south.

"What about you?" Captain Tang asks.

If you're on the trail, you won't have to worry about ever fighting your brother's ARVN unit. But you also want to fight in your homeland, to help it reunite with the North.

58

To go to the Ho Chi Minh Trail, turn to page **69.**

To stay in South Vietnam, turn to page **71.**

"I'll go with you." The student smiles and tells you his name is Trang. He takes you to meet his older brother, Hien.

"The Viet Cong is like any army," Hien explains. "It needs intelligence to learn what the enemy is doing. When you can, go to where the Americans work and live. Talk to the Vietnamese who work for them. Learn from them what the military is doing. If anyone gets suspicious, lie to them. Even lie to your aunt, if you have to. We must do anything to win!"

At night you begin going to bars where Americans go. You talk to the Vietnamese girls who sit with them. You say to one, "If you hear anything about what the army might be doing, let me know."

Turn the page.

"Why?" she asks. "Are you some kind of spy?"

"No," you lie. "I support President Diem and the Americans. I'm just curious about the war."

She walks away. But you wonder if you're making a mistake. You don't know anything about gathering intelligence. As you start to leave you see the girl return—with an ARVN soldier!

"You," the soldier calls out. "Come here."

You approach the soldier, and he grabs your arm. "Why are you asking so many questions?"

"My brother is in the army," you say. "I never hear from him. I just wanted to know what was going on."

"Come with me," the soldier says. He begins dragging you down the street. Maybe he will take you to a military office and question you. But most likely he will torture you because he thinks you are with the Viet Cong. You wish you had never left your home and come to Saigon.

THE END

To follow another path, turn to page 11.
To read the conclusion, turn to page 101.

"Sir, I'd rather not see the wounded and dying all the time."

The next day your unit attacks a nearby Viet Cong camp. U.S. helicopters fly out ahead of you to fire at the enemy. Ground troups also fire artillery at the camp. You receive an order to enter the camp. The Viet Cong sometimes set up booby traps, so you watch for punji sticks in the ground. These sharpened bamboo sticks can pierce your body. As you approach the camp, the Viet Cong begin to fire mortar shells. One lands near you, and you see several ARVN soldiers blown to bits. The shelling continues, and you feel dazed and sick.

You've had too much of this war. As the fighting goes on all around, you decide to desert. Many South Vietnamese have deserted, and more do as the war has gone on.

You sneak away and head back to your village. But you know soldiers will look for you there. You'll have to keep moving, perhaps toward Cambodia. You don't know if you'll ever be able to return home for good.

THE END

To follow another path, turn to page 11.
To read the conclusion, turn to page 101.

A U.S. Marine shows one of the booby traps used by the Viet Cong.

"I would be honored to treat wounded fellow soldiers," you tell the captain. He smiles and tells you to get ready for the trip to Saigon.

In Saigon you train at the Military Medical School. You also go out to villages with U.S. military doctors to treat the sick there. This is part of a program to win support from the villages so they'll be less likely to support the Communists.

Your training is almost done by January 1968. As the month comes to an end, you prepare to celebrate Tet, the Vietnamese New Year, with your Aunt Ly. The Viet Cong celebrate it too, and they call for a break in the fighting. On the morning of January 31, though, you hear explosions in the city. The Communists are attacking Saigon!

Your first thought is to make sure Ly is safe. You leave your apartment as more explosions go off around you. You hear gunfire too, as U.S. and ARVN troops fight back against the attackers. As you turn the corner onto Ly's street, an artillery shell explodes near you. It kills you instantly.

THE END

To follow another path, turn to page 11.
To read the conclusion, turn to page 101.

"I'm no soldier," you say. "I'm just a farmer."

"You're a fool," a Viet Cong leader says. "You should fight for your freedom!"

The soldier goes over to another farmer, Nguyen, who begins pointing at various men. Other Viet Cong approach these men and force them at gunpoint to leave the village.

"What's happening?" you ask your father.

"Nguyen must be working for the Viet Cong! And now they're taking away anyone who strongly supports the ARVN. To the Communists, anyone who helps the government is a traitor."

One of the men being led away is an old farmer named Loc. He has several sons in the army, but so do many of the farmers. You run over to the Viet Cong who is taking him.

"He's just an old man. Leave him alone."

"Mind your own business," the fighter says.

"No!" You reach out toward him. The fighter swings the butt of his rifle at you, knocking you to the ground.

"Stay there if you know what's good for you," the fighter says. Loc looks at you as he leaves the village. You see a tear in his eye.

A few seconds later, you hear gunshots. The Viet Cong have killed all the men they took away! You hear the screams of the wives and daughters of the men who have just been killed.

Your father pulls you up. "You could have gotten killed too! We should just mind our own business."

Turn the page.

You say nothing, but you know what you must do. The first chance you get, you'll head to the ARVN base and join the army so you can fight the Viet Cong. You don't want any more men like Loc to die for no reason.

THE END

To follow another path, turn to page 11.
To read the conclusion, turn to page 101.

"The trail is important for winning the war," you tell Captain Tang. "I'll volunteer."

Captain Tang, you, and a dozen men drive in small trucks toward Laos. Your group arrives at a part of the trail that is still being expanded.

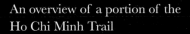

An overview of a portion of the Ho Chi Minh Trail

The route is much more than a trail through the woods. It's wide enough for trucks to travel in both directions at the same time. Long lines of North Vietnamese military trucks and artillery are heading south.

You reach a camp in the jungle where you will live. Tang explains that your job is to make repairs to the road after the Americans bomb it. They began bombing the trail in 1964.

"We must work hard," says Tang. "The traffic must keep moving along the trail!"

That night you hear something overhead. You look up and see American bomber planes. Bombs fall as you and the other men run for cover. A bomb explodes near you, killing you instantly.

THE END

To follow another path, turn to page 11.
To read the conclusion, turn to page 101.

"I'd like to stay with my unit, sir," you tell Captain Tang. He simply nods and walks away.

You finally head out for battle in November 1965. The ARVN control hills in the Ia Drang Valley. Your commanders want to force them out. Soon thousands of Viet Cong and North Vietnamese forces head to the valley. You learn that many American soldiers are in the region too.

At first your troops have success fighting the ARVN. But as the Americans arrive with their powerful helicopters, the battle becomes much harder. U.S. planes also bomb your position.

Turn the page.

After several days of deadly fighting, the Viet Cong and North Vietnamese soldiers retreat toward Cambodia. Your company is helping protect a field hospital as it moves to safety. But there is no hiding from the U.S. helicopters, which spot you.

You fire your gun at a helicopter even as it fires much more powerful machine guns and rockets. Explosions erupt all around you, and you hear the screams of wounded men nearby, but you keep firing. Suddenly you feel bullets pass through your shoulder. You drop your gun and fall to the ground. Finally, after causing heavy damage, the Americans leave.

You're lucky that you were traveling with the hospital. Medical personnel immediately bandage your wound. Many others, however, weren't so lucky. They were killed in the attack. You're glad that you survived, so you can fight again to help liberate your country.

THE END

To follow another path, turn to page 11.
To read the conclusion, turn to page 101.

A 1968 antiwar protest in New York City

CHAPTER 4

To Fight or Not?

It's the summer of 1968, and you've recently graduated from high school. In the fall you'll work in your father's machine shop. Most of your friends, though, will be going to college.

"It's the easiest way to get a deferment," your friend Bobby says. "I don't want to be drafted and get sent to Vietnam."

Like other young men, you and Bobby registered for the military draft on your 18th birthdays. More than a million young men have been drafted since you started high school. But guys like Bobby, who go to college, can delay getting drafted.

75

Turn the page.

The deferments have not stopped many young people from protesting the war. The first major protests began in 1965. On TV you saw young men burning their draft cards. They did this to show they opposed the war and didn't want to go to Vietnam. Several thousand young men burned their cards even after Congress made it illegal.

You believe it's wrong to kill people who don't pose a direct threat to the United States. But you never protested the war. You couldn't be sure that North Vietnam didn't pose a threat to South Vietnam and the region. The war, though, has been going on much longer than people hoped.

President Lyndon Johnson had announced on March 31, 1968, he would not run for president again, largely because of his failure to win the war. He also announced the start of peace talks. That means his party, the Democratic Party, has to choose a new candidate for president at its summer convention in Chicago.

"There are going to be huge protests against the war in Chicago," Bobby tells you one day. Bobby has gone to several local marches to protest the war.

"My sister and I are going to Chicago," Bobby says. "Will you come with us?"

You could be arrested if you protest. But you know Americans are dying in Vietnam. You could soon be one of them.

To go with Bobby, turn to page **78.**

To stay home, turn to page **80.**

"I'll go," you say. "But what will I tell my parents?"

Bobby explains that he and his sister Rosemary are going to stay with an aunt who lives just outside Chicago. She has room for you too.

That night you tell your parents about Bobby's invitation to go with him and Rosemary to Chicago. They think it's a great idea for you to travel before you start working. You don't say anything about the protests.

You, Bobby, and Rosemary take the train and reach Chicago on August 25. The convention starts the next day. At times it feels like a party. Thousands of protesters fill Lincoln Park and listen to bands.

Thousands of police and National Guard are in the city too. Police helicopters circle overhead. The police will arrest people who disobey the law or become violent. When the park closes for the night, the police order the protesters to leave. Some refuse. You see a cloud of smoke fill the air, and your eyes start burning.

"It's tear gas!" Rosemary says.

"Should we run?"

"I came here to protest the war," Bobby says. "You can run if you want, but I'm staying."

"Me too," Rosemary adds.

You see police swinging their clubs at the protesters. But if you leave your group, you'll be alone in a big, strange city.

To stay with your group, turn to page **82.**

To run, turn to page **86.**

"No, I think I'd better stay home," you tell Bobby. "My parents want me around for the summer."

As Bobby leaves, you go out for the mail. There's a letter addressed to you—from the U.S. government. With your hands shaking, you open it.

"ORDER TO REPORT FOR INDUCTION," it says on the top. You know what that means—you've been drafted!

You show your parents the notice. Your father had served in the military, but like many others, he thinks the Vietnam War is wrong.

Your mother agrees. "But if you don't report," she says, "you'll be arrested!"

You go see a group in town that helps inductees resist the draft. Burt is the man who runs the group. He has long hair and wears glasses.

"It's your decision," he says. "But you wouldn't be here if you didn't think the war is wrong."

"It is wrong," you say. "But I'm not sure I want to get into trouble."

To choose to be inducted, turn to page **84.**

To resist the draft, turn to page **96.**

"Let's stay together," you say. "But be careful!"

You wipe away the tears from your stinging eyes. One teen near you yells, "Stay in the park! Parks belong to the people."

"Come on," Bobby says. He grabs Rosemary and tugs at you to join them in the crowd. You see more police lined up, holding their clubs. The city's mayor, Richard Daley, had promised that the protesters wouldn't disrupt the Democratic convention. You hear some of the protesters yell at the police. Angry cops begin chasing them. Soon the police swing their clubs at anyone on the street.

Bobby points to one officer who is beating a woman.

"We should try to stop him," you say.

"No, let's just keep with the crowd," Bobby says. "What could we do anyway?"

Bobby is probably right. The police officer is huge, and there are others around him. But it seems wrong for him to beat a woman.

To help the woman, turn to page **88**.

To stay with Bobby, turn to page **90**.

Police got physical with protesters as they cleared out Grant Park in Chicago during the 1968 Democratic National Convention.

"My mother's afraid I'll get arrested," you tell Burt.

"It's your choice," Burt says. "You could always flunk the induction test—on purpose."

"What do you mean?"

Burt explains how some people avoid the draft by failing the various tests. "Some make scars on their arms and pretend they shoot drugs. Others give the wrong answers on the intelligence tests. And some inductees even break their own bones to get out of serving!"

84   "I don't want to do anything like that," you say. You don't think you could lie to avoid the draft.

The day comes to go to the induction center. When you arrive, young men and women are marching on the sidewalk with signs. Some say, "We Won't Go!" Others say, "Stop the War!" One of the protesters comes over to you.

"Don't do it," he says. "Do you really want to be a tiny piece in a huge killing machine?"

You don't want to kill anyone. If you don't go inside the induction center, you could show that you oppose the war. That's what Bobby is doing in Chicago. But do you have a right to avoid the military when so many other men are being sent to Vietnam?

To go in for your induction, turn to page **92**.

To join the protesters, turn to page **94**.

"You guys, this is crazy," you say. "Let's go."

"We're staying," Rosemary says, as she and Bobby run off into the crowd.

You leave the park and search for the train station. You plan to stay there overnight and find Bobby and Rosemary in the morning. While you walk, you see more police everywhere, swinging their clubs. Some of their targets are protesters, but others are local people who just happen to be outside.

Suddenly, you feel something smack into the back of your head. You've been hit! You fall to the street, bleeding. A man comes out of his apartment and pulls you to his front steps.

"We'd better call an ambulance," he says, "There's a lot of blood."

Blaring sirens fill the air as police attack the protesters. You hope your friends are OK and you'll see him tomorrow at their aunt's. You understand why people oppose the Vietnam War. But protesting against it is something you'll never do again.

THE END

To follow another path, turn to page 11.
To read the conclusion, turn to page 101.

Police with clubs attack protesters in Grant Park during the 1968 Democratic National Convention.

"I have to do something," you say. "Come on."

Bobby and Rosemary follow as you approach the cop and the woman, who's bleeding.

"Stop!" you yell. "What did she do to deserve a beating?"

Another cop approaches you. "Maybe you should just mind your own business. Or better yet, spend a night in jail for interfering with an officer."

The man's large, beefy arm reaches out for your neck. Before you can pull away, he grabs you and drags you to a nearby police wagon.

"Bobby!" you try to yell, but almost no sound comes out. With a look of terror, Bobby calls out, "Don't worry! I'll tell my aunt. She'll get you out."

The cop throws you inside the wagon. Seconds later, the woman joins you. She's crying.

"What did you do?" you ask.

"I just tried to help someone getting beat up by the police," she says. "They shouldn't treat people this way."

You nod. And you wonder what a night in jail will be like.

THE END

To follow another path, turn to page 11.
To read the conclusion, turn to page 101.

Most of the people are leaving the park. Bobby and Rosemary agree to go too. You take the train to their aunt's house and spend the next few days there. Then on Wednesday you, Bobby, and Rosemary head back to downtown Chicago.

Protesters are marching to the building where the Democratic National Convention is taking place. Inside the Democrats choose Vice President Hubert Humphrey as their candidate. He says he will continue President Johnson's policies on Vietnam. This angers Democrats who want the war to end now.

In the streets some protesters throw tomatoes and stones. Some of them even try to kick in the doors of police cars. You smell more tear gas as the police respond with force, wildly swinging their clubs.

The scene sickens you. You turn to your friends.

"Let's go. This is too crazy for me."

"Yeah," Rosemary agrees.

"I'm glad we leave tomorrow," Bobby says.

The next day on the train home, you wonder what waits for you. Maybe a draft notice. You might see violence of another kind soon, in the jungles of Vietnam.

THE END

To follow another path, turn to page 11.
To read the conclusion, turn to page 101.

You ignore the protesters and head inside. Despite what Burt told you, it just seems wrong to lie or do anything else to try to fail the tests.

In a few weeks, you get the final word: You passed all your tests and you'll be reporting for Army basic training. The war is wrong, you think, but you did the right thing by not lying. You just hope you get a job in the Army that keeps you in the States. You don't want to be one of the soldiers who is seriously wounded or killed in Vietnam.

THE END

To follow another path, turn to page 11.
To read the conclusion, turn to page 101.

THIS IS NOT A PUBLIC ENTRANCE. AD-
MITTANCE PERMITTED TO SELECTIVE
SERVICE REGISTRANTS ORDERED TO
REPORT BY THE LOCAL BOARDS, AP-
PLICANTS REFERRED BY THE RECRUIT-
ING SERVICES, PERSONNEL ASSIGNED
TO, OR EMPLOYED BY THE AFEES.
ALL OTHERS USE THE 1515 CLAY
STREET ENTRANCE.

E COME
IN
PEACE

PULL PULL

Vietnam War protesters try to urge
drafted men not to report for duty.

"I don't want to be part of this war in any way," you tell the protester. "What can I do?"

"You can apply to be a conscientious objector. Do you have religious beliefs that keep you from trying to kill anyone?"

You and your family aren't that religious, so you don't think you'd be considered a conscientious objector.

"Nope. Anything else?" you ask.

"Some of the inductees are going to burn their draft cards today. You can join them."

You take your card out of your wallet and look at it. "I'll do it!" you say.

By now a local TV crew has come to film the protest. Some police have shown up too. You feel your legs go weak as someone passes you a lighter so you can torch your card. This could get you arrested. But you don't care. You want to make a public statement against the war.

You hold on to the card as it starts to burn and then drop it to the ground. More young men burn their cards or their induction letters. Then you feel a tight grip on your arm. You turn and see a police officer.

"You're under arrest," he says. You get into a police car, not knowing what will happen next. But you feel good that you have taken a stand against a war you oppose.

THE END

To follow another path, turn to page 11.
To read the conclusion, turn to page 101.

You think a few minutes. "I'm not going to go to my induction appointment," you tell Burt.

"Good," he says. "But you don't want to risk being arrested, do you?" You shake your head. "Then you should think about going to Canada."

You've heard about young men who go to Canada or Sweden to avoid the military. The U.S. government considers them criminals for refusing induction. Like those so-called draft dodgers, you could be arrested if you go to Canada and then return. But you're willing to take that chance.

You go home and tell your parents you're not going for the physical exam, and you're heading to Canada instead. Your father doesn't like the idea of your ignoring the induction notice.

"Do you want him to die in Vietnam?" your mother asks. "Or go to jail?"

Your father grumbles, but says nothing more when you leave the house with some clothes. You find Burt, and he helps you buy a bus ticket.

"Good luck," he says. "You'll do fine."

After a long ride, the bus pulls into Toronto, Canada's largest city. Burt had given you the name of an organization that helps young Americans fleeing the draft. Once you're in Toronto, a woman named Carly tells you her group can help you find a job and a place to live.

"Do most guys like me like it here?" you ask.

"Some of them are lonely at first," Carly says. "It's hard to leave your friends and family behind. But once you get a job and make some friends, I think you'll be all right."

Turn the page.

You look at the woman and try to smile. You miss your parents already. But you didn't want to go into the army or go to jail. You tell yourself you made the right decision. Still, you hope there will be a day when you can legally go back to the United States.

THE END

To follow another path, turn to page 11.
To read the conclusion, turn to page 101.

SELECTIVE SERVICE SYSTEM

Approval Not Required.

ORDER TO REPORT FOR
ARMED FORCES PHYSICAL EXAMINATION

THE LAW —
requires you to appear
personally to answer
roll call at this office
at the scheduled time.

LOCAL BOARD NO. 1
124 W. MAIN ST.
SMITHTOWN
NEW YORK 11787

(Local Board Stamp)

To Mr. Anthony J. Chliek, Jr
10 North Ingelore Court
Smithtown, New York

March 1, 1968

(Date of mailing)

SELECTIVE SERVICE NO.			
30	1	48	2664

Dear Mr. Chliek:

You are hereby directed to present yourself for Armed Forces Physical Examination to the Local Board named above by reporting at:

LOCAL BOARD NO. 1
124 W. MAIN ST.
SMITHTOWN
NEW YORK 11787

(Place of reporting)

on March 8, 1968 at 7:30 a.m.
(Date) (Hour)

Marie M. Dascole Marie M. Dascole
(Member or clerk of Local Board) mc

IMPORTANT NOTICE
(Read Each Paragraph Carefully)

TO ALL REGISTRANTS:

When you report pursuant to this order you will be forwarded to an Armed Forces Examining Station where it will be determined whether you are qualified for military service under current standards. Upon completion of your examination, you will be returned to the place of reporting designated above. It is possible that you may be retained at the Examining Station for more than 1 day for the purpose of further testing or for medical consultation. You will be furnished transportation, and meals and lodging when necessary, from the place of reporting designated above to the Examining Station and return. Following your examination your local board will mail you a statement issued by the commanding officer of the station showing whether you are qualified for military service under current standards.

If you are employed, you should inform your employer of this order and that the examination is merely to determine whether you are qualified for military service. To protect your right to return to your job, you must report for work as soon as possible after the completion of your examination. You may jeopardize your reemployment rights if you do not report for work at the beginning of your next regularly scheduled working period after you have returned to your place of employment.

IF YOU HAVE HAD PREVIOUS MILITARY SERVICE, OR ARE NOW A MEMBER OF THE NATIONAL GUARD OR A RESERVE COMPONENT OF THE ARMED FORCES, BRING EVIDENCE WITH YOU. IF YOU WEAR GLASSES, BRING THEM. IF MARRIED, BRING PROOF OF YOUR MARRIAGE. IF YOU HAVE ANY PHYSICAL OR MENTAL CONDITION WHICH, IN YOUR OPINION, MAY DISQUALIFY YOU FOR SERVICE IN THE ARMED FORCES, BRING A PHYSICIAN'S CERTIFICATE DESCRIBING THAT CONDITION, IF NOT ALREADY FURNISHED TO YOUR LOCAL BOARD.

If you are so far from your own Local Board that reporting in compliance with this Order will be a hardship and you desire to report to the Local Board in the area in which you are now located, take this Order and go immediately to that Local Board and make written request for transfer for examination.

TO CLASS I–A AND I–A–O REGISTRANTS:

If you fail to report for examination as directed, you may be declared delinquent and ordered to report for induction into the Armed Forces. You will also be subject to fine and imprisonment under the provisions of the Universal Military Training and Service Act, as amended.

TO CLASS I–O REGISTRANTS:

This examination is given for the purpose of determining whether you are qualified for military service. If you are found qualified, you will be available, in lieu of induction, to be ordered to perform civilian work contributing to the maintenance of the national health, safety or interest. If you fail to report for or to submit to this examination, you will be subject to be ordered to perform civilian work in the same manner as if you had taken the examination and had been found qualified for military service.

SSS Form 223 (Revised 4-28-65) (Previous

All young men in the United States received an induction notice when they turned 18.

President Richard Nixon uses a map to discuss the Vietnam War on television.

1. CEASE FIRE

2. PEACE CONFERENCE

CAMBODIA   SOUTH
                           VIETNAM

3. WITHDRAWAL TIMETABLE

4. POLITICAL SOLUTION
                    Saigon
5. PRISONER RELEASE

CHAPTER 5

A Long and Costly War

Richard Nixon was elected U.S. president in November 1968. He said he wanted "peace with honor" in Vietnam. He said South Vietnamese troops should do more of the fighting. They received more military aid from the United States, and U.S. troops began coming home.

Nixon also ordered more bombing of Communist bases in Cambodia. That prompted intense protests on college campuses across the United States. Still, a peace treaty between North Vietnam and the United States was not signed until January 1973.

The war cost many lives. Slightly more than 58,000 Americans either died or went missing during the war. More than 300,000 were wounded.

After the U.S. combat troops left, the South Vietnamese still battled the Communists. Nixon had promised South Vietnam continuing military aid. The American people and Congress, though, were tired of the war in Southeast Asia. The lawmakers cut back on military aid. The North and South Vietnamese continued to fight until the Communists won the war in 1975. Between 1965 and 1975, across all of Vietnam, about 3 million people died because of the war.

U.S. President Gerald Ford offered amnesty to draft evaders in September 1974. They would not be punished if they took jobs helping the public.

In 1977 President Jimmy Carter pardoned all who had evaded the draft. Men who had left the country would not be punished if they returned.

The end of the Vietnam War did not end debate about the American role in it. Some scholars thought U.S. leaders ignored the deep desire of many Vietnamese to end foreign influence in their country. U.S. leaders also feared they would be criticized by some Americans if they did not stand up to Communist nations.

Some military leaders claimed the United States could have won the war by expanding the fight into North Vietnam. But President Johnson in particular did not want to risk directly bringing the Soviet Union or China into the war by doing that.

The Vietnam War also sparked a huge movement of people from Southeast Asia to the United States. By 2010 the United States was home to 2.5 million people who had come from Vietnam, Cambodia, and Laos. Some left Vietnam after that country improved its ties with the United States.

President Bill Clinton started official relations with the Communist government there in 1995. Two years later Douglas Peterson arrived in the Vietnamese capital of Hanoi to become the first U.S. ambassador to the Socialist Republic of Vietnam. He, like many other Americans who served in the war, went back to the land where he had fought many years before.

The people who came to the United States from Asia after the Vietnam War were called "boat people" because they often came on crowded boats.

TIMELINE

1945—Ho Chi Minh declares Vietnam's independence from France.

1946—France and Vietnam go to war; the French receive a great deal of aid from the United States.

1954—Vietnam wins its independence and is divided into a Communist north and a democratic south.

1957—The Viet Cong, with help from North Vietnam, begin their attempt to reunite Vietnam under Communist rule.

1961—South Vietnam begins creating strategic hamlets across the country to defend against Viet Cong attacks.

1963—South Vietnamese president Ngo Dinh Diem is killed by his own generals; about 16,000 U.S. military advisers are serving in South Vietnam.

1965—First U.S. ground combat troops arrive in Vietnam; first big antiwar protests begin in the United States, which include young men burning their draft cards.

1966—U.S. Marines begin County Fair, a program designed to win the support of South Vietnamese civilians.

1968—In January Viet Cong forces attack Saigon and other cities and military installations over the Tet holiday; in March President Johnson announces he will not seek re-election because of the war; in August police and antiwar protesters clash in the streets of Chicago.

1969—President Nixon orders a secret bombing of Cambodia, which will last 14 months, without the knowledge of Congress or the American people; huge antiwar protests take place in Washington, D.C.

1970—Secret peace talks begin.

1972—Nixon cuts troop levels in Vietnam; secret peace talks are revealed.

1973—The United States and North Vietnam sign a peace treaty, but the north continues to battle South Vietnam.

1974—President Gerald Ford offers amnesty to young men who evaded the draft.

1975—The Vietnam War ends with the Communists in control of the whole country.

1977—President Jimmy Carter pardons all men who evaded the draft.

1995—The Socialist Republic of Vietnam and the United States open official relations with each other for the first time since the end of the war.

OTHER PATHS TO EXPLORE

In this book you've seen how events from the past look different from three points of view. Perspectives on history are as varied as the people who lived it. Here are ideas for other points of view to explore.

American women served in the military in Vietnam during the war, mostly as nurses. If you were a nurse during those years, would you volunteer for the military? What kind of conditions would you experience in Vietnam? (Common Core: Key Ideas and Details)

As the Vietnam War ended, many people in Southeast Asia wanted to escape the Communist governments in South Vietnam, Cambodia, and Laos. Many fled on overcrowded boats. Would you choose to risk your life to live in a new country? What would life be like as a refugee? (Common Core: Integration of Knowledge and Ideas)

The countries that sent troops to help the United States and South Vietnam battle the Communists were called the Free World Military Forces. Some of the troops came from Australia. If you were an Australian then, how would you feel about your country's role in Vietnam? Would you protest the war, as many Americans did? (Common Core: Integration of Knowledge and Ideas)

READ MORE

Jeffrey, Gary. *The Vietnam War.* New York: Crabtree Publishing Company, 2013.

Senker, Cath. *The Vietnam War.* Chicago: Heinemann Library, 2012.

Spilsbury, Richard. *Who Protested Against the Vietnam War?* Chicago: Capstone Heinemann Library, 2014.

INTERNET SITES

Use FactHound to find Internet sites related to this book. All of the sites on FactHound have been researched by our staff.

Here's all you do:
Visit *www.facthound.com*
Type in this code: 9781476541877

GLOSSARY

amnesty (AM-nuh-stee)—an official pardon or forgiveness for breaking the law

artillery (ar-TIL-uh-ree)—cannons and other large guns designed to strike an enemy from a distance

communism (KAHM-yuh-ni-zuhm)—a way of organizing a country so that all the land, houses, and factories belong to the government, and the profits are shared by all

court-martial (KORT MAR-shuhl)—a trial for members of the military accused of breaking rules or committing a crime

deferment (di-FUR-muhnt)—an approved postponement of required military service

guerrilla (guh-RIL-ah)—one of a group of soldiers who strike at the enemy in small numbers and then quickly retreat

hot LZ (HOT EL-zee)—a landing area for a helicopter that is coming under enemy fire; "LZ" stands for landing zone

infantry (IN-fuhn-tree)—soldiers trained to fight on the ground

medic (MED-ik)—a soldier trained to treat the wounded; Navy medics were known as corpsmen

BIBLIOGRAPHY

Fails, William R. *Marines and Helicopters, 1962–1973.* Washington, D.C.: History and Museums Division Headquarters, U.S. Marine Corps, 1978, 1979.

Karnow, Stanley. *Vietnam, A History.* New York: Viking, 1991.

Kusch, Frank. *All American Boys: Draft Dodgers in Canada from the Vietnam War.* Westport, Conn.: Praeger, 2001.

Li, Xiaobing. *Voices from the Vietnam War.* Lexington: The University Press of Kentucky, 2010.

Luan, Ngyuyen Cong. *Nationalist in the Viet Nam Wars: Memoirs of a Victim Turned Solider.* Bloomington: Indiana University Press, 2012.

Merrill, Dennis, and Thomas G. Paterson, eds. *Major Problems in American Foreign Relations. Vol. 2: Since 1914.* Boston: Houghton Mifflin, 2000.

Pratt, John Clark, ed. *Vietnam Voices: Perspectives on the War Years, 1941-1982.* New York: Penguin Books, 1984.

Santoli, Al. *To Bear Any Burden: The Vietnam War and Its Aftermath in the Words of Americans and Southeast Asians.* New York: E.P. Dutton, 1985.

Summers, Harry G. *The Vietnam War Almanac.* New York: Presidio/Ballantine Books, 1999.

INDEX